# UNITY

# UNITY

## The Highest Form of Evangelism

## Dr. David W. Hopewell, Sr.

Unity
The Highest Form of Evangelism

Copyright © 2008 by Dr. David W. Hopewell, Sr.

ISBN 10: 0-9786056-1-6
ISBN 13: 9780978605612

All Scripture quotations, unless otherwise indicated, are taken from the King James Version of the Bible.

Printed in the United States of America
Published by The Joshua Ministry
1772 Enid Drive
Lithonia, GA 30058

# DEDICATION

This book is dedicated to my late pastor, Dr. George O. McCalep, Jr. I will always be eternally grateful to him for bringing me on staff in the position of Minister of Evangelism. He not only gave me the opportunity to develop my God-given gifts, but also inspired me to write and publish. I appreciate his leadership, godly example, and most of all for accepting me as a son.

# ACKNOWLEDGMENT

All glory goes to God for the inspiration to write. I thank my wife for thirty years of support and encouragement. I thank Geraldine Jones, Judy Hollis and Faith Management Service for their help in editing this publication.

# TABLE OF CONTENTS

# INTRODUCTION

Since my first publication "The Joshua Ministry-God's Witnessing Army," www. Joshuaministry.com, I have been consumed with the state of the Body of Christ relative to our responsibility to the Great Commission- and those things which hinder us from fulfilling that commission. Many churches are exerting great efforts in reaching the lost and fulfilling the Great Commission. I truly and sincerely applaud their efforts. However, I am somewhat disturbed with those things which hinder our witness and divide us as a body; they are: Prejudice relative to race, other Christians, and prejudice against the lost. In my opinion, these three areas hinder our witness, hinder us from working together as brothers and sisters in Christ, and hinder our witness to the lost.

I am more convinced than ever that the lack of unity within the body of Christ not only hinders our witness, but also hinders the return of the Lord. Jesus clearly prayed for the unity of His followers (John 17), which will be discussed later. Secondly, according to the writings of the apostle Paul found in (Eph. 4:11-13), the five-fold ministry gifts - apostles, prophets, evangelists, pastors, and teachers, were given to the church to perfect Her till we all come in the unity of the faith. This has not occurred to this point, and very well may be hindering the return of the Lord!

What you are about to read is what God has stirred in my heart. I do not know how well I can communicate this truth, but I trust God will use this publication to open all of our eyes and bring healing and unity to His body. I believe with all my heart that if I had not written and published this book, I would have been disobedient to God.

The contents of this publication is not intended to be a theological debate, but simply what God has placed on my heart. I cannot express the conviction, passion, and urgency within my heart to convey this with the entire body of Christ. It is my hope that every church and denomination leader will grab the content of this book and communicate it in your own theological context, tradition or language. I pray that before we cast aside, or criticize its content, we will ask God to open our eyes and give us understanding.

# CHAPTER ONE
## Jesus' Prayer for Body UNITY

We probably all can agree that much can be achieved when people work together in unity for the same cause. When I think of people working together for one cause, two select passages of Scripture come to mind. The first is found in Genesis chapter 11, the Tower of Babel. The second is found in Nehemiah 4:6, where it says, "and the people had a mind to work." Both passages demonstrate what can be achieved when people intentionally come together, in unity, with the same purpose, and a mind to work. These Scriptures indicate their willingness to work together, and their ability to achieve the task. Actually, if God had not intervened in the Genesis passage, they would have achieved their task and built a tower that reached heaven. What was it about their efforts that aroused God and got His attention? I believe it was the oneness they displayed. There was no division in their purpose or effort. The Scripture says "behold, the people are one" (Genesis 11:6). I would like to believe this oneness, or unity, caught God's attention, and resulted in a personal visitation from him. Before this visitation from heaven, the only other visitation from God to man was with Adam (Gen. 1-2). God had appeared to Adam in the cool of the evening and had fellowship with him. However, there is no suggestion of fellowship or relationship between God and those in the Genesis 11 account. Yet, the mere fact that they worked together and would have achieved their task, got God's attention, and he responded from heaven. I would like to strongly suggest, that before this time, God had paid little attention to those in the Genesis 11 text. I would like to suppose the unity they displayed got His attention because it displayed the same unity which was displayed in heaven between the Godhead, and the unity He expressly desired to be proven to a dying world before the return of Christ. I believe unity is what God desires for His body. As I stated in the introduction, the five-fold ministry gifts, apostles, prophets, evangelist, pastors and teachers, according to Eph. 4:11-13, are to equip or teach the "body" until she walks and lives in unity. The five-fold ministry gifts are to teach us, until we all come into the unity of faith, and into the knowledge of the Son of God, unto a mature man. The unity or oneness Paul spoke about would bring us to a place that we are persuaded and rely upon Christ for salvation. Unity would mean that we are full age. Aside from this, I do not know what that entails. Will it mean we agree on all points of doctrine, procedure, or policy? Probably not; however, it does mean we are to unify in what the Ephesians passage calls, "the unity of the faith."

The "unity of the faith" could mean different things to different believers, however, I would like to suggest for your consideration, what I believe the "unity of the faith" could be. I believe the "unity of the faith" is not the name of any denomination, church, or Parachurch ministry. Rather, the "unity of the faith" is the common "faith," we share in Jesus, and what He provided through his sacrificial death at Calvary. The death and resurrection of Jesus are the exclusive events that unite us as one. The resurrection is the one single event that unites all orthodox churches, catholic churches, and protestant churches. The cross is the single event that should unite us and our work in God's kingdom. The unity that we display should have such an affect that it draws the unbeliever beneath the Savior's cross. The result of our prayer is directly related to the prayer Jesus prayed before his death, and what He expected to occur.

In John 17, Jesus prayed an interesting prayer. What is the significance of this prayer? More than anything, this was His request before His death. This prayer is the longest in the New Testament. He was expressing His last desire that we unify. My oldest son David said about this text, "When I think of one, no one can be greater then any other part." Jesus said He and the father were one. How can we effectively fulfill the Great Commission if we are not one with each other and with Jesus and the Father? We cannot fulfill the work if we do not know God; God is love, and if we do not love, we do not know God, nor can we communicate his message effectively. Jesus was going away from them and was placing them in the care of His Heavenly Father. The prayer was a prayer of intercession in which He prays for himself, the disciples, and those who would believe in the message of the cross, based on the disciples' preaching, and those beyond the disciples' influence who would preach the message of the cross. His prayer was not self-centered. It could have been, and who would have blamed him? He was going to die, so why not pray selfishly? It is not like He had no knowledge of the impending events which were about to occur. Yet, His prayer included others. He first briefly mentions Himself, but He quickly moves beyond His desire and need and begins to pray for those who were around Him, his disciples. He could have only prayed for those who had been supportive to His ministry, and those who had been with Him from the beginning and were eyewitnesses of all He said and did. However, His prayer reached beyond the disciples to all who would hear the message of His death and accept its invitation to discipleship. His prayer included those who had not been born yet, those in the future. It included you and me.

The first request Jesus made was that He be glorified. He expressly desired to be restored with the glory He laid aside when he robed himself in humanity. According to Phil. 2:6-7, He laid aside His divinity and came in the likeness as man. Second, He prayed that the disciples be sanctified or set apart for the use of God. Jesus prayed that God would keep them from the world. They were to be in the world but not part of the world. He wanted them to be kept from the evil of the world (John 17:6-19). Thirdly, He prayed for those who would, down through history, believe on the message of the gospel. His prayer was that those who believed, received the message, and became His disciples would come to a place of unity. This unity would have such an impact on the world that the lost would know that God had sent Him. The direct result would be that the world would know without a doubt He was sent by God! The effect would be that unity between the members of His body, would witness to the world that Christ is the answer. The church has yet manifested such unity. This unity is displayed between Him and the Father, and based on His prayer, should be in us. The world should see in us, invisible form, the unity that exists between Jesus and the Father. This unity should bring us together in thought, purpose, and action relative to the Great Commission. I believe the church, the body of Christ, at this point, is fragmented and this type of unity alludes us. If this is true, then we are fragmented. How then can we bring healing to others if we need healing ourselves?

God's intent has always been to have a chosen people. Israel was God's first choice, however they stumbled at the righteousness of God through Christ (Rom. 9). Yet, Paul goes on to explain that they will be grafted into Christ at some point. At this point God has extended His grace to all who believe in and accept exclusively Jesus, and salvation through him alone. The Church was chosen after

Israel rejected the Messiah. The church will fulfill God's intent; Jesus guaranteed it! Jesus said "the gates of Hell will not prevail against it." (Matt 16:18). This Scripture assures the success of the church and its unity. Paul wrote about unity in I Corinthians 12, and Ephesians 4. In his letter to the church at Corinth, Paul addresses those things which hinder us from operating in unity. In the twelfth chapter, he describes how a fractional body should operate when all components are in their proper place, doing what they were made to do. It seems that Paul understood unity, and its effect relative to its function. When members of the body function apart from each other the body can never function as it was designed. Paul gives an example of that in I Cor. 12.

The prayer of Jesus found in John 17 reflects Jesus, heart felt desire to see his church demonstrate and exemplify what He, the Holy Spirit, and the Father epitomize daily in heaven, unity. Paul, in Ephesians 2:15-16, expands on unity to include the Jews making one new man in one body! Again, His prayer was three-fold, that he would glorify his father; the disciples would be sanctified, and for those who believe on Him through the disciples would come to a place of unity. The unity Christ prayed for is of the highest importance, for without unity our witness is hindered. The church in the book of Acts seems to understand and live out His desired prayer for unity.

Discuss the significant nature of John 17 prayer and its relevance today.

_____

_____

_____

_____

_____

_____

_____

_____

_____

_____

_____

_____

_____

_____

_____

_____

_____

Without hesitation, I believe the church in the book of Acts lived out Jesus' prayer, and the results were compelling. What made the early Church so successful in reaching the lost? Some suggest obedience, I agree, to some extent. Yet, beyond their obedience I point to their unity. The question I raise is: Would the same results have occurred if all 120 disciples had gone back to Jerusalem and gone into their separate homes? Jesus' command was that they go back to Jerusalem and wait. He never told them to wait together at the same location, in unity. He did pray that they come together in unity (John 17:11). Perhaps this was a fulfillment of His prayer in John 17. I believe the greater results of Pentecost were not their obedience alone, but their unity. They could have been obedient, but still not together in one place all seeking the same results. No doubt, every Christian, every church and denomination would probably say, or at least think they are obedient to God and His purpose for their church. Yet, the "body" is not unified. The question I raise is: Are our results equivalent to those of the Acts church? I am not saying we as a "body" are not doing great things, but are we doing supernatural things—are we manifesting the same results as the Acts church did as an infant? Three thousand souls were added at one time, 5,000 on another occasion shortly thereafter (Acts 3 and 4). Some may argue, the church is producing the same results. To defend this, some would point to thousands of decisions that are made for Christ at crusade services during modern times, especially in third world countries. I agree. However, results of this proportion, as much as I can ascertain, have not been produced by the post-modern day church, but by individuals or single ministries.

I do not believe it is God's intent for the world to be won to Christ by one person, one church, one ministry, or Para-church ministry, but by His body coming together in unity as one.

There were four results which were by-products of what occurred in Acts chapter two. These results particularly affect non-believers. First, fear came upon every soul (Acts 2:43). Second, wonders and signs were done by the apostles (vs. 43). Thirdly, God gave the believers favor (vs. 47). Lastly, God added to their number daily those who were being saved (vs. 47). Unity preceded these results. There are repeated places in Acts chapter one and two where unity is displayed. It is interesting that the words "all" and "they" appear several times in the first two chapters. In fact, "all" appears twenty-one times and the word "they" appears twenty-two times. Let's examine the times unity was displayed. Surely with so many references to unity, we must consider its importance and without fail consider that God couched it within these two chapters for a reason. This is the birth of the church! This is the infant, the baby, and she produced extraordinary results as we read within this book. If this was the baby, what will the adult look like and what will she produce? As an infant, the church proclaimed the gospel, cast out devils, healed the sick, shared, prayed together, stood together against critics, conducted business, and worshiped together, all in unity.

As I stated above, there are at least forty-three times the church in Acts one and two operated in unity. Let's look at some of them. The first time we see unity displayed is in the first chapter, verse 6.

"When they therefore were come together, they asked of him, saying, Lord, wilt thou at this time restore again the kingdom to Israel?" Notice, it could have said one of them said, but it said all of them said. Verses 9 and 10 refer to them looking up together as He was taken from them. All looked, not just one. Verse 12, "Then returned, they unto Jerusalem." Not one but all together returned. Verse 13 indicates that when they came in, they all went in an upper room; verse 14 says that **all** of them continued with one accord in prayer and supplication. In verse 13 the names of the disciples are listed, and verse 14 indicates that other women and Mary, the mother of Jesus, was included. Chapter one closes with the appointment of Matthias. There is no indication of division as they proceeded through His process of selection. No one was upset and collected their ball and bat to go home because their candidate was not selected. Notice the unity as they selected and affirmed God's selection. In verse 23 they appointed two men. Verse 24 says they prayed over their selections and in verse 26, they cast their lots. They conducted church business in complete unity! Chapter two opens with the Day of Pentecost. They were all on one accord in one place. They were all sitting (verse 2). Cloven tongues sat upon each of them (verse 3). They were all filled with the Holy Spirit, and began to speak with other tongues as the Spirit gave utterance. In verse 13 the crowd responded by mocking this event, "These men are full of new wine," they said. As the church was under attack, or persecuted, the disciples did not side with their persecutors, or talk about what occurred within their ranks, or what took place in worship, or church business, but responded in one voice. In verse 14 Peter stood up **with the eleven** and said, "Fellow Jews and all of you who live in Jerusalem, let me explain this to you; listen carefully to what I say." What we could accomplish if we all had one voice. We could get things done, change decisions within city government and school system. When Peter began to explain what occurred, those who mocked were pricked in their heart and asked, not Peter only, but all of them, "men and brethren what shall we do?" They were all baptized (verse 41), and 3,000 souls were added as they heard the message. "They continued in the apostle's doctrine, fellowship, breaking bread, and prayers." All that believed were together, and had all things common; they sold their possessions and distributed them to all men, as they had needs. They continued daily in worship (verse 46), fellowshipping together from house to house, and praised God together. They all contributed to the needs of others, they all attended prayer meetings. They were not selective as to what service they would attend, if any, but all attended together (verse 46). As they came together and worshiped, they all participated. Their unity did not go unnoticed or unrewarded, God responded. Their unity produced heavenly results. "Fear came upon every soul," (verse 43), signs and wonders were preformed (verse 43), God gave them special favor (verse 47), and God added to the church daily. Although results occurred due to unity, I chose to highlight the results relative to evangelism. I believe as we demonstrate a whole body before the world, it will communicate the gospel without us saying one word. The world will know by our unity that God sent Jesus and He is the one and only way of salvation (John 17: 21-23). The results will be the same as it was in Acts 2:43-47, with the greatest result being the addition of souls that will enter the kingdom of God. I believe the Acts church knew this and acted it out daily. Somewhere we have gotten away from unity. As the church progressed though the ages, especially when denominations came about, the body has become more divided.

I believe denominationalism, or mode of thinking, has inhibited the unity that was lived out among the early church and from that which God intended for us to display. I am not saying denominations are inherently evil. Denominations have done, are doing, and will continue to do ministry, deploy missionaries, and be a safe-haven for many. Yet, they have also hindered our working together and our witness to the world. Although we have diversity within our denominations we should do all we can to not allow it to bring division between us, especially as it relates to the Great Commission. Yet, the things that divide us have taken our focus off the main thing, the Great Commission. I am not saying they are not of significance, however, in light of someone being saved, a life changed, a person being transformed from the kingdom of darkness to the kingdom of God, these differences are less significant.

Discuss the Acts church model and its significances today.

_____

_____

_____

_____

_____

_____

_____

_____

_____

_____

_____

_____

_____

_____

_____

_____

_____

# CHAPTER THREE

**Hindrances Within the Body**

A t times our denominational mode of thinking causes more divisions and have caused paramount problems within Christendom. How can we attribute this mode of thinking as something from God when it has divided us so? The Bible clearly teaches that God is not the author of confusion. Yet, this mind-set has left the sinner confused as to what form of religion is correct, and has kept us from the main thing, the Great Commission. The lost I come in contact with, before sharing the gospel with them, converse about denominations, not Christ. Satan presents unity in great diversity in such things as music, porn, violence, corruption, etc. These things are not confusing to them. These are things that hinder the sinner. Why so many denominations and why so many different beliefs from one denomination and church to another? This does not exist between those things Satan presents to them as an alternative to church. When I say church I mean just that, church, not Christ- because the sinner usually does not reference Christ, but the church and the people who attend. The differences and hypocrisy of the church hinder our progress to reach the lost.

According to Ephesians 6:12, Paul describes an order of command in Satan's army: principalities, powers, rulers of darkness of this world, spiritual wickedness in high places. He is describing the order of Satan's kingdom, not God's. It would seem that Satan's kingdom is more organized than God's kingdom. Years ago, my youngest son had a teacher who, at one time belonged to a Christian church. At some point she decided to join the Jehovah's Witness church because, as she said, "the church has so many different beliefs from one congregation to another that they don't know what they believe; at least the Jehovah's Witness know what they believe." We not only believe different beliefs from one church to another, but we also demonize each other before each other and the world.

Churches and their members talk about other churches and ministries with no regard to weak Christians or unbelievers who may be listening. I have heard professors, preachers, and seminar speakers talk about other preachers and ministers as though they were the enemy. I am not saying that I am not without guilt. However, we are family and should pray for our brothers and sisters. We seem to demonize others who are not of the devil, but born of God. The mere fact that their doctrine is more liberal or conservative than what you or I believe, does not mean they are of the devil. In fact, if they believe exclusively that Jesus died and rose from the grave for their sins and they have accepted Him, they are our brothers and sisters in Christ (Rom. 3:23-25).

It is because of His blood we are one. If there is some misinterpreted Scripture, we should be willing to come along side of our brothers and sisters and expound to them the more excellent way, not disown them as a brother or sister. I believe this common belief in Christ is the key to the unity of the faith and should propel us to work together as Christian brothers and sisters, yet, our corporate witness will be hindered as long as we remain fragmented. Most of us have not presented Christ to the lost but denominational traditions that have nothing to do with salvation. My youngest son D'Andre said, "Dad how can someone enlist someone to be on a team if they are not on the team?" What a simple but profound question. What are you or your denomination presenting to others relative to salvation? Is it biblically communicating salvation or tradition?

There are both obvious and subtle things that prevent unity in the body of Christ. No doubt, race plays a big factor, and race is not limited to one ethnic group alone. The lines of race and the spirit of prejudice is among all groups to some degree. Great strides have been made to over come racial barriers, yet the struggle continues both outward and inward. The most obvious struggle is demonstrated during our Sunday morning services, which suggest segregation within our congregations is a part of the gospel, at least this is what some may ascertain by our display of division. We are communicating a separate God for each ethnic group. When we witness only to those who look like we do, we segregate the gospel. The command of Jesus to go to Jerusalem, Judea, and Samaria (Acts 1:8), and to the highways and hedges (Luke14:23), to share the gospel, suggest we go to all ethnic groups, not just our own. If we only concern ourselves with those of our own persuasion, our witness is only a Jerusalem witness. The world is not going to be won by one church or one denomination, but by one body who may have different names, but unify around Christ, His message, and the Great Commission, and will not allow doctrinal differences to separate us. These differences communicate a message of division and disunity. God is not divided nor confused, can we truly say this is of God?

Paul seemed to understand unity and how the body should react as different gifts function in one body. Paul spoke of a body of gifts, not denominations. Each part of the body was a gift, placed in the body as God desired. What would be the reaction of the world if they saw not a display of denominationalism, but a display of different gifts all functioning for the good of the body? The following diagram illustrates this.

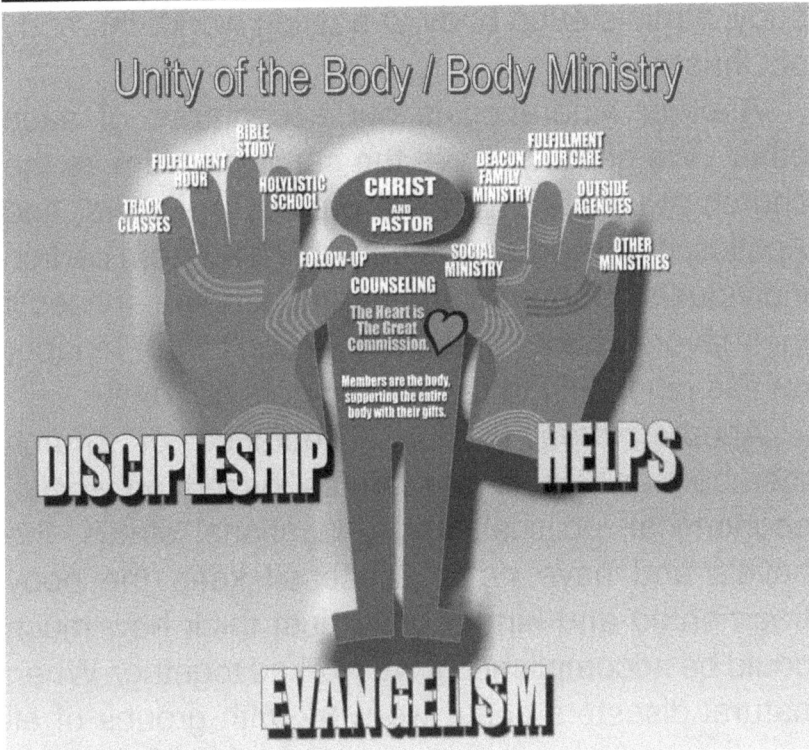

Unity of the Body / Body Ministry

BIBLE STUDY
FULFILLMENT HOUR
HOLYLISTIC SCHOOL
TRACK CLASSES
CHRIST AND PASTOR
FULFILLMENT HOUR CARE
DEACON FAMILY MINISTRY
OUTSIDE AGENCIES
FOLLOW-UP
SOCIAL MINISTRY
OTHER MINISTRIES
COUNSELING

The Heart is The Great Commission.

Members are the body, supporting the entire body with their gifts.

DISCIPLESHIP

HELPS

EVANGELISM

1. The head represents Christ.

2. The neck represents counseling.

3. One hand represents discipleship.

4. The other hand represents ministry.

5. The heart represents the Great Commission.

6. The knees represent prayer.

7. The feet represent evangelism.

The body should represent members who function in their gifts, and support the entire body. These gifts could also be replaced by denominations that bring to the table their giftedness, or their area of specialization, all making up a complete functioning body, a ministering body to a dying world, the body of Christ.

Another hindrance is our acceptance of each other. We seem to have the same problem as the church at Corinth; we have our Pauls, Peters, and Apollos, our favorites. We can only hear from certain individuals. Some will not attend certain services if their favorite is not preaching. I don't want to labor on this point, just to say this hinders our unity.

Another area is our acceptance of church members, which is sometimes based on social, economical, political, and educational status, the have's and have not's. These all keep the body fragmented and hinder unity. Just think how much could be accomplished if we worked together. When natural disasters occur we work with groups of all races, vocations, social, economic, and financial statuses. Could it be that catastrophic events unify us but kingdom work does not? These hindrances directly affect our witness, our working together, and the harvest that awaits us. When we conquer these hindrances, the dying world will witness a living Savior.

I see "unity" as the highest form of evangelism. Perhaps the question raised is, "Why did Jesus give us the Great Commission if unity would produce a greater harvest of souls, and reveal a higher form of evangelism?" Valid question, I can only say, **maybe, I am not saying this is truth,** but maybe God knew the body of Christ would be divided, hindering the harvest. Rather than wait for the body to come into unity, He established the Great Commission until the body unified.

Unity is a great force seen in Scripture, examples of good and evil both exist as stated earlier. Unity produced great results as people worked together.

I propose "unity" is the highest form of evangelism. I am not discounting our current efforts, nor am I suggesting we discontinue our current efforts to reach those held by the bondage of sin. However, I am suggesting we unify so we may witness the greatest harvest of souls ever known. The current disunity within the body of Christ indicates a working power among us, but not from God. It would almost seem the kingdom of Satan is more unified than God's church. Jesus prayed for unity in John 17, and I believe he will get His prayer answered. I hope that God does not have to use something catastrophic to bring us into a place of unity.

Discuss the Acts church model and its significances today.

_____

_____

_____

_____

_____

_____

_____

_____

_____

_____

_____

_____

_____

_____

# CHAPTER FOUR

## Hindering the Harvest

efore offering solutions there is one other hindrance worth discussing. This hindrance is not within the body, or what hinders the church, but some things which hinder the harvest from being reaped. There are things that the church, or that the Christian does that hinders the harvest from being reaped. One of the greatest hindrances to receiving the harvest is hypocrisy. As we encounter numerous people who are lost, we hear story after story about how church people live among the lost. In most cases we live no different than they do. I understand this because I was hindered from receiving Christ as a direct result of this same hypocrisy. Just like the lost, I thought, "Why should I change my life and accept Christ if I can continue doing the same things?" Jesus called one that lived in this manner a hypocrite!

In the book of St. Luke (6:39-42) Jesus said, "Can the blind lead the blind?" In this particular book, I see three things occurring. One, Jesus on mission, seeking and saving the lost; second, training the disciples, and third, the response of the church. Jesus is training the disciples in the passage found in St. Luke 6:39-42. He is teaching them that they can not catch a lost person if they are living the same way they live. He calls this type of lifestyle hypocrisy.

Another prejudice or hindrance is how the saint treats the sinner. Just as saints discriminate against other saints based on education, social, economical, political and others; we do the same to sinners. On Father's Day in Atlanta, a prostitute was walking down the street and heard music coming from a church. The Spirit of God through the music begins to draw her and she decided to enter the sanctuary and participate in worship. As she entered the vestibule, an usher denied her entrance because she was a prostitute. The good thing about the story is that she went up the street and found a storefront church that accepted prostitutes, drunks, those on drugs, and every other type of lifestyle some churches refuse to accept. I was told on another occasion that a church had an evangelism problem and needed advice. The problem was, and I quote, "We have large numbers of teens that live next door to the church in an apartment complex and they are coming over to our church, and we do not want them at our church." A pastor from another city called me and told me he desired to hold an outdoor service to reach the lost in his community. As he planned the service, he sent a letter to a church in the neighborhood that he was going to hold the service, since there was no place to hold the service where his church was located. The pastor invited the church to participate, but he received no response. After holding the service he was so excited about the results but received a phone call that almost caused him to leave the ministry. On the other end of the line was an area supervisor from his denomination. You would have thought that he would have shared in his excitement; however, that was not the case. Rather, he was told that the pastor from the church he had sent the letter to wanted to know why he was in his neighborhood, and that he needed to stay on his side of town. Another church began to transport teens from the inner city to their worship service. Some of the church members accepted and embraced them while others were cruel and made comments about their dress and body odor. On one occasion one of the members cursed at two boys and told them to pull their pants up. The boys said they would never return to the church again. A few months later I inquired about the two boys and found out that one of them had been shot in the head and killed. I could not help but think that maybe the church had some responsibility in his death. Perhaps he would have taken a different direction or been at church, I can not say.

Robert Lewis, in his book, **Church of Irresistible Influence**, says the church has burned down bridges to the community she was called to reach. I say it another way. Have you ever had a neighbor that fails to keep their property up? They are the unwanted neighbor in the neighborhood. The church has become the unwanted neighbor in the neighborhood. The status of yester-year that the church had is no longer recognized. The church used to be the safe haven in the neighborhood. The church and preacher were respected. The church was the voice not only in the community, but even presidents and kings looked to the church for direction. The current status of the church is one of disdain, the unwanted neighbor in the neighborhood.

I have personally witnessed churches and their treatment to homeless persons who come by for help. I have witnessed members treating the lost different based on their appearance or condition of life. I have witnessed church members who did not want to take the time to help a new member based on their appearance. I have heard those who visit our churches, turned off to the point that they have no desire to visit again. I have witnessed the apathy towards those who live in urban communities. We act as if certain parts of our cities are Hell itself. One street person told me that the church was a pimp and the neighborhood a prostitute because the church never comes to the community until she wants something. By these examples, some churches decide who is acceptable to them or not. When we should be celebrating the lost receiving Christ most members look at them as if they were a disease. This behavior is not something new, Jesus experienced the same.

As we go back to the book of Luke we can see some of the same examples. For example, the Scribes and Pharisees are church members. The publicans are Jews who collected taxes for the Romans, and the sinners are Jews who did not keep the law. On one occasion (5:27-32) Jesus sees a publican named Levi, who He invites to follow him. Levi is so excited that he prepares a feast and a great company of publicans and others come over. If you allow me to use my imagination, Jesus is the pastor and Levi becomes his convert. Levi is so excited that he invites other unsaved friends to come over for a block party. You would think the members of the church would have been excited. You would think they would have prayed for their salvation, and minister to their needs. Their response is found in verse 30, "Why do you eat with publicans and **sinners**?" The members had their own exclusive club and sinners were not welcome. I thought this was about sinners coming to Christ, fulfilling the Great Commission. Another example is a Pharisee (church member) who desired that Jesus (pastor) would come over to his house and eat. A woman who was a **"sinner"** (7:36-39) brought an alabaster box of oil and began to wipe His feet with her hair. You would have thought the church member would have been happy that Jesus would have had an opportunity to minister to her. Yet, his response was, "If he was a prophet (pastor for our illustration) he would have known what kind of women this is, because she is a sinner!" These accounts demonstrate us driving away or killing the harvest.

Everyone has worth, and needs to be loved accepted, and valued. When we can share the love of God with someone, accept them right where they are in life, value them as a person, and help them to discover worth within, then the harvest will respond. My daughter D'Lisa shared with me that, "people will not hear us or our message if we do not make them feel comfortable. Unless we take down the mask and become real, expose our wounds to some degree, people will not hear us. It is when we do this it brings people into the same circle as us, unity, and they will hear us." Some of our churches need to learn how to receive the harvest. Why should God give us a harvest if we are going to drive it off or kill it? We need to love everyone, accept them where they are, value them as God's creation, and understand they have worth. They have potential, God has made them for a purpose and we must help them discover it. In the story of the demoniac (Mark 5) Jesus recognized something that neither the towns people nor his disciples recognized. This man had worth; He looked at him through the eyes of faith. He did not see his current state, but what he could become. There is also something else missed while preaching this text. The demoniac was not just cutting himself, but was also crying. Jesus saw that even though a demonic spirit was trying to kill him, he was crying out for help! On one hand a spirit of death and suicide was trying to end his hope of a changed life. On the other hand, he desired help! He had the same potential of any of his disciples. Jesus not only saw him trying to kill himself, but saw him calling out for a change, something no one else saw. What do we see when we look at the lost? Do we see pants hanging down, a drug addict, and a prostitute? Do we prejudge the sinner based on their appearance or lifestyle? We must look beyond what we see and accept all and not act like gate keepers. "It would be better that we have a stone around our neck and be cast into a sea than if we offend one of these little ones" (Luke 17:2).

What are some things that hinder unity within the local church today and how should we address them?

_____

_____

_____

_____

_____

_____

_____

_____

_____

_____

_____

_____

_____

_____

_____

I was always told that a poor preacher is one who can raise a problem, but give no solution. So, I want to give some solutions so we can move more aggressively towards unity.

## Pray for unity

I think that if Jesus can pray for unity, we should too. We need to add this request in our daily and corporate prayer. Along with praying for the lost, I do not see any prayer more important. However, it must be out of a sincere heart. We need to pray that we have one voice. We need to pray for the lost and that God would help us meet their needs.

## Teach unity

We need to follow Paul's example and teach unity. It is important that we teach members the purpose of the five-fold ministry gifts that are in the "body." Along with teaching (Ephesians 4) we should teach the importance of the gifts and how they function and comprise one body, the body of Christ. According to the Ephesians passage, we are to teach members of the body until unity occurs. I believe it is important that we begin to communicate the message of unity to our congregations. Passages such as I Corianthians 12 and Ephesians 4 would be a good start.

## Intentionally work together for kingdom building

We must work together. We are to build God's kingdom, not our own. In our quest to work for "the praise of His glory," we must first seek to embrace our differing gifts and expertise. These are not merely for our own gratification, but must be employed for the sake of the Great Commission. In other words, whatever various gifts or insights we have within the body are to be used toward fulfilling the Great Commission. Could it be that the differing gifts and grace given to all of our churches and traditions are all needed to fulfill the Great Commission? Could it be that our fragmentation prevents a greater display of His glory from being shown to the world?

There exists far too much bickering about the legitimacy of our gifts and areas of knowledge. I propose that our differences should not be debated. Rather, if any church or tradition feels that they have gifts, they should be brought to the table in fulfilling the Great Commission. If another tradition feels that they have been entrusted with guarding sound doctrine, this should be brought to the table to help keep us focused on fulfilling the mandate of our Lord. If another tradition feels that they have a greater understanding of parish and how to care for their community, this knowledge should be shared in helping to fulfill the Great Commission.

Our differences held in debate and segregated do nothing in fulfilling the Great Commission. It is only when we bring our various flowers together for cross pollination that we see new life birthed. On the other hand, those things that in truth hold no legitimacy in God's kingdom and cannot be substantiated by Scripture will undoubtedly fall away in complete impotence as we engage the world. There will be no need for one tradition to critique another when we bring what we have to the table. Whatever is of no consequence will simply be exposed for what it is as we move out unified in the Lord's work.

This requires humility and openness. It could very well be that certain practices we find theologically discomforting are in fact of great use in fulfilling the Great Commission. On the other hand, there may be certain things we hold dear that are exposed as completely ineffective and illegitimate as we move together in fulfilling the Lord's work. The greater point here is that we need not argue over what we have or what we practice. What is needed is to bring all these things to the table together in fulfilling the Great Commission. When we do this, we will be surprised to find that certain areas of lack we have in our churches can be filled by our brothers and sisters from other traditions. When we do this, we will also find ourselves corrected by each other. Whether we experience correction or enhancement, we will find ourselves better and actively involved as one in the service of our Lord. As I write this, I am reminded of Paul's words to Timothy as it relates to the Scriptures in 2 Timothy 3:16-17. Paul said, "All Scripture is given by inspiration of God, and is profitable for doctrine, for reproof, for correction, for instruction in righteousness: That the man of God may be perfect, thoroughly furnished unto all good works." In the same way we, the body, are given to each other for purposes of doctrine, reproof, correction and instruction so that we might move toward perfection. This will only happen, however, as we come together and bring what talents, gifts, expertise and experience to the table in seeking to fulfill the Great Commission.

We have to get to the place that all the praise and glory go to God and not ourselves. This appears to be the problem at the Tower of Babel and ours today. Everyone can not be in charge. We are all on the same team, playing for the same coach, building the same kingdom, against one foe. Remember what my son said, "how can we bring someone on the team if we are not part of the team?" We must examine the reason we don't work together and begin to work past those things that hinder us. The world waits for the manifestation of the sons of God (Rom. 8:19) but we continue to demonstrate a fragmented body and hinder the harvest.

## One Great Day of World Evangelism

Recently we had our first ever "One Great Day of Connection," which is properly known as "One Great Day of World Evangelism." The vision is that of Minister Jeanette Cody, a member of Greenforest

Community Baptist Church where I am a member. We both received strategies at the same time, but it was not until recently that I have come to an understanding how they work together. The Lord has given her a strategy that the body of Christ unites together on the day before Easter and share the gospel with a lost person or invites a lost or un-churched person to church. Churches can elect to have a block-party, evangelize door-to-door, or anything they choose as long as the objective is to win the lost. This one event would then be followed by a seven-month effort of seedtime and harvest. In other words, the church would go on the offense and continue to reach out and evangelize and minister to the lost and un-churched with great intensity for a period of seven months. I do not know what occurs after the seven months. Some would be so excited about witnessing that they would continue. Perhaps Jesus would come back after our efforts, something to think about. If you want to learn more about "World Day Evangelism" or sign up to participate, contact our website at www.joshuaministry.com.

Name additional things that hinder the harvest from being reaped?

_____

_____

_____

_____

_____

_____

_____

_____

_____

_____

_____

_____

_____

_____

_____

_____

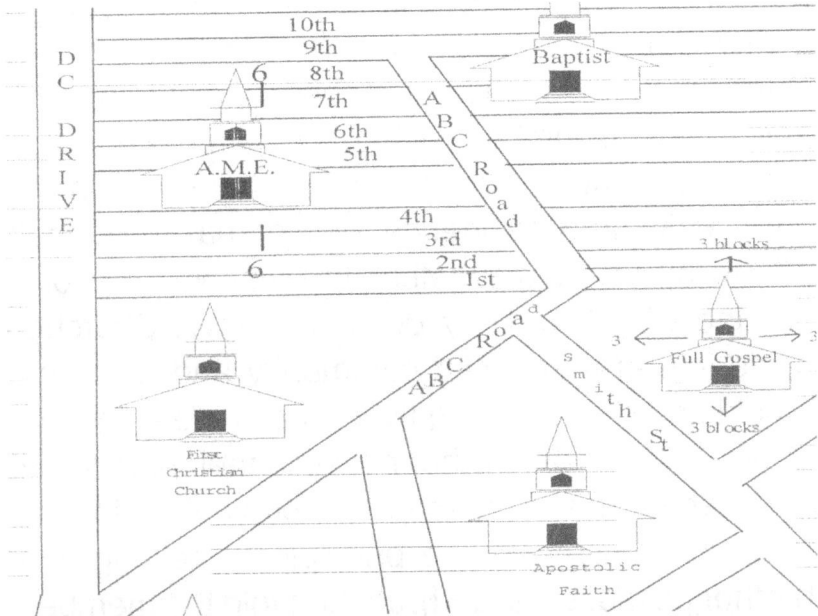

I believe each city regardless of size can be evangelized in one year. If each church, having the common ground of salvation exclusively through faith in the blood of Jesus Christ, would come together, divide the target neighborhoods into blocks, and go street by street, door by door, block by block, sharing the gospel and meeting needs until the next assigned area is reached. Each city could be evangelized in one year. This strategy will only work as we come together as one unit helping others possess their land. This means that although we possess different labels, we unify under the Lordship of Jesus, salvation exclusively through him, and the Great Commission. Regardless of our differences, these, in my opinion, are the three most essential places of commonality. Each church would be responsible for a twelve-block area in which they would share Christ and meet needs through their resources, not exclusively money, but para-church ministries, other churches, and government agencies. Churches within the same zip code, because of the common interest they share in the community and residence, could maximize their efforts by working together in unity. We are only sharing Christ and not doctrinal views. Churches could join in a selected community and represent a host church- repeating the same process in other areas, helping each other possess their land. Read more about this strategy in my book **The Joshua Ministry,** (based on the principle of helping your brother possess his land). Joshua told the members of the tribes of Reuben, Gad, and Manasseh to cross over the Jordan River and help their brothers possess their land. The tribes of Reuben, Gad, and Manasseh desired their inheritance on the other side of the river and were only allowed their inheritance if they crossed over and helped their brothers possess their land (Joshua 1:13, 14). Moses understood that a joint effort would yield the greatest results. You can read more about this strategy and other strategies in the Joshua book and Implementation Manual by visiting www.joshuaministry.com .

## House Church Strategy

In my office I have drawn a circle representing I-285, the interstate which goes around the city of Atlanta. Through that circle I have lines which represent I-75, I-85, and I-20. Both I-75 and I-85 go north and south, I-20 east and west. I have taken a marker and indicated in green the location of our church, and another color marker places where we have existing home Bible studies. My son D'Juan and I were talking about this; he has a passion for ministry in the inner-city. He was sharing how our strategy could involve other churches. We also talked about becoming incarnated within a community. The principle was demonstrated by Jesus as we stated above, where He left his divinity and took upon himself the likeness of mere man. It means becoming part of that community. The church would be involved in every aspect of the community. The ministry of the church would become holistic in nature ministering to the whole man; spirit (the spiritual man), soul (the mind or education), and body (the physical part). We could work together by planting a house church in a home or apartment complex. As the resident lives there and develops relationships, ministers to needs, is involved in all aspects of the community as a resident in the community, he or she will be fulfilling the following passage from Isaiah 32:2-3.

*"As we become a hiding place from the wind for the residence; and as we become a cover from the tempest, and a shadow in a weary*

*land. Then their eyes will be open and they will hear us."*

As we develop the people we would solicit the help from trained associates who are waiting for an opportunity to minister. Ministers would come from churches of different denominations but have as a point of unity, salvation in Christ. This process would then be duplicated in another area, and then another until the entire city was affected. I do not know how long this would take. Some may feel this is too simplistic, yet God has chosen the simple things.

I hope this publication, while not lengthy, may be found refreshing and have an impact that moves us all to unity! I have shared what I believe is God's desire for His church. I believe this is something we can obtain if we commit ourselves to God first, each other, and the work that awaits us. Let us begin by agreeing with Jesus and pray for unity and each other. Let us stand united together in force against the enemy that divides us for the glory of God.

How can this strategy work within your community? Whom can you begin to work with to fulfill this strategy, thus fulfilling John 17?

_____

_____

_____

_____

_____

_____

_____

_____

_____

_____

_____

_____

_____

_____

_____

_____

# UNITY STRATEGY
**For Homeless**

The following represent a strategy for reaching the homeless population in our communities. The following Scripture suggests others will hear us when we become a hiding place from the wind and a covering from the tempest. Those who followed David and became mighty men (1 Samuel 22: 1-2) were in distress, discontented, and had no money, like the homeless. Like David's men, if we care, nurture, develop and prepare the homeless, they can too.

> 1 David therefore departed thence, and escaped to the cave Adullam: and when his brethren and all his father's house heard it, they went down thither to him.
> 2 And every one that was in distress, and every one that was in debt, and every one that was discontented, gathered themselves unto him; and he became a captain over them: and there were with him about four hundred men.
> **1 Sam 22:1-2**

1 Behold, a king shall reign in righteousness, and princes shall rule in judgment.

2 And a man shall be as an hiding place from the wind, and a covert from the tempest; as rivers of water in a dry place, as the shadow of a great rock in a weary land.

3 And the eyes of them that see shall not be dim, and the ears of them that hear shall hearken.

**Isaiah 32:1-3**

## Vision Statement

Our vision is to see the church eradicate homelessness in America's cities en route to fulfilling the Great Commission. By clustering homeless persons in family housing units, connecting homeless persons with social services already in existence and providing personal, holistic ministry, we will fulfill the design of Isaiah 32:1-3. In so doing, the expected result will be discipleship followed by the cultivation of new leadership.

## Mission Statement

Our mission is to provide for the two most pressing needs of homeless persons- housing and discipleship. We seek not to institutionalize the homeless, but to provide for their housing and holistic needs, facilitating their transition to self-sufficiency. All of this will be done in obedience to Christ.

## Goals

• To foster Christian discipleship among the homeless.

- To cultivate new Christian leadership for the purpose of discipling others.
- To facilitate the reintegration of homeless persons into the mainstream of society
- To assist homeless persons in transitioning to self-sufficiency.
- To help homeless persons take advantage of all resources already available in regards to housing, food, medical care, job training and job placement.
- To assist homeless persons in transitioning to permanent housing.
- To move toward the eradication of chronic homelessness in American cities.

**Objectives**

- Each church, or ministry that participates will receive information relative to the Adullam project.
- Each homeless person will be discipled.
- Each homeless person will be assimilated into the mainstream of society.
- Each homeless person will be trained and assisted as they transition to self-sufficiency.
- Educate the homeless population of resources available to them.
- Each participanting church or ministry will be invited to be discipled in the Adullam model.

Each church can use and certainly build on what is presented here within their own community. We would hope and pray that each church take on this project and fund it from your church or ministry. The church can do this without the support of the government. In fact, the Scriptures promise blessings and to those who consider the poor, read them (Ps. 41:1, 112;9, Pro. 19:17, 21:17).

## Action Steps

1. Solicit cooperation and commitments from parachurch organizations,shelters and all other Christian outreach groups actively providing services to the homeless.
2. Solicit cooperation of several churches throughout the city of all denominations that have a burden for fulfilling the Great Commission.
3. Come to a firm agreement as to the scope of the pilot project.
4. Secure a registry of potential house stewards. Ideal candidates would be willing to live in houses with clients or be able to commit substantial time to them. Ideal candidates would be single. Ideal candidates would be church staff persons, associate ministers, seminary students or parachurch staff persons.
5. Have potential house stewards undergo training/education of all pertinent social services and resources available for potential homeless clients.
6. Identify potential housing units for purchase/rent.
7. Negotiate and purchase housing units.

8. Finalize selection of house stewards and accountability measures between them and participating local churches.

9. Use parachurch organizations servicing homeless clients to identify prospective subjects for pilot.

10. Screen and select pilot subjects and place them in housing units.

## Target Population

For a test pilot initiative we would like to target single homeless individuals. We would like first to start with subjects defined as less at risk. This would include persons without any history of mental illness or alcohol and drug abuse. In addition, persons with prior felony convictions would not be ideal for the pilot run. This would leave people who are simply homeless as a result of social factors; lack of affordable housing, low wages, underemployment or victims of unforeseen circumstances.

## Timeline

The entire timeline from initial contact with potential partners to actual implementation will be 24 months. Once subjects are moved into the half-way home, we assist them by providing love, discipleship and existing services. Their goal is to locate their own permanent housing. The target time range for doing this will be 18 months. During this time subjects will have acquired steady employment, vocational skills, and a supportive community. In addition, each month they would have contributed to a savings account to be used for several months of rent or a down payment on their own home.

## Theological Foundations

In our culture, there exists a general attitude of resentment toward Christians. I believe this is rooted in our own hyprocracy. We are in large part faithful only to the proclamation of the gospel message while neglecting the demonstration of it. Followers of Christ in our country have historically understood this. The church was the engine behind the abolitionist, the civil rights, the women's suffrage and the child labor movement. In addition, many of our schools, universities, hospitals and relief organizations were birthed out of the church in obedience to Christ.

Jesus told his followers to let their light shine before all men so that in response to seeing our good works, they would glorify our Father in heaven (Matt. 5:16). His followers were told to do as he did, feeding the hungry, healing all who are sick, and oppressed of the devil (Matt. 10:8). Furthermore, Isaiah 32:1-3 indicates that when followers of the great King are viewed as shelter from the wind, refuge from the storm and streams of water in the desert, then those who are blinded to the truth will see and their ears will be open to hear our message. In obedience to this, we must become the shelter for the least of these and the refuge for those lost so that the proclamation of the gospel might be received.

In all of our efforts as the church, both individual and universal, we must continually allow the Scriptures to be our guide. We must come together in obedience to Jesus' last will and testament in fulfilling the Great Commission so that the world might know Him (John 17). We must unite, not in the name of our churches or for our own glory, but in obedience to Christ and for the praise of His glory. Finally, we must not fall prey to the same delusion Israel did in the 8th century B.C. In all of their religious activities and rituals, God was not pleased. God made it clear that he despised their festivals and religious assemblies (Amos 5:21). God answered the people and made it known that he desired justice (Amos 5:24) and that the people would bring the homeless poor into the house (Isaiah 58:7).

## Rationale

Despite the relative prosperity enjoyed in America during the 1990's, homelessness today has actually increased from the levels of the 1980's. On any given day, it is estimated that the number of homeless persons in America could exceed 800,000. Agencies and organizations recognized as providing assistance to homeless persons are mostly proficient in assisting the homeless in just that—being homeless. This is unsettling. Although the federal government is beginning to realize the need to provide housing and transitional assistance to homeless persons, historically the emphasis was placed on emergency shelters. As recently as 2000, only 44 percent of HUD's competitive homeless funds used for housing and services were used for housing activities. The result has been the institutionalization of the homeless populace. Further, those agencies receiving funding are compensated more as their numbers increase; the more people held in the facility, the more money is received.

Years of research conducted by various institutions and foundations has emphatically concluded that the cost to society to hold transients in their position far exceeds the cost of providing housing. This is particularly true for those with mental health and substance abuse issues. A 2002 study by New York's Coalition for the Homeless found that:

**"Permanent housing for homeless families and individuals costs less than shelter and other emergency care**. The cost of sheltering a homeless family in the New York City Shelter system is **$36,000 per year**, while the cost of shelter for a homeless individual is **$23,000 per year**. In contrast, a **supportive housing apartment** with services costs as little as **$12,500 per year**, and **rental assistance** with support services for a family costs as little as **$8,900 per year.**"

Our nation's historical course of action for servicing the epidemic has merely produced an ever increasing homeless population along with its social and monetary costs to society. On the other hand, helping people into housing, whether permanent or transitional, not only is proven to be more cost effective, but actually helps move toward eradicating homelessness. If history is to be our guide, we can no longer afford to use fruitless strategies from the past in the future. If Scripture is to be our guide, we can by no means afford to neglect a primary mandate and not confront all evils in our society rooted in sin. We must act in unity in a way that is both truly meaningful and effective. We can accomplish this if we come together. We can make this happen in our cities. We can all contribute a portion of our resources, time, talent, and treasure. This can be accomplished by the church not government grants. We can learn from those who labored towards the completion of the Tower of Babel and those who built the wall during Nehemiah's time. However, more critical is the fulfillment of Jesus' prayer in John 17. As His body, let us strive to fulfill His prayer.

What are some additional ministry projects that would need the support of other members of the body?

_____

_____

_____

_____

_____

_____

_____

_____

_____

_____

_____

_____

_____

_____